Praise f

Octogenarian on Fire

"For 15 years we have relished Vilma Ginzberg's poetry and prose, and now, in *Octogenarian On Fire*, she plumbs again her seemingly bottomless reservoir of inspiration and energy to surface with ever-new treasures. Vilma's new book will challenge, stimulate, and satisfy her many readers, and show how, at age 90, she continues to embody creative force and spirit that the rest of us can only envy. Her poems exemplify craft, originality and vision, as well as what all lasting poetry seems to have: empathy and authenticity. Thank you Vilma! These are poems to absorb, savor, honor, and read again and again."

—David Beckman, author of *Language Factory of the Mind*

"If you want to know a real human being, read these poems. If you want to walk with Vilma Ginzberg, talk with her, let her take you, barefoot, across her fields and through her wooded hills into the land of her experience, know that you might well throw away your disguises and wear your true face."

—Clare Morris, author of *Love Poems to the City*

"Vilma Olsvary Ginzberg blazes the truth of what is indispensable and being lost...equally full of outrage that cuts to the quick and compassion that binds the wounds....fiery bright in dark places....hearth fire words of loving warmth, slow glow gratitude, grief underneath outrage....celebrating earth's core burn from which life grows. It's a wonder this book does not combust in our hands!"

—Shashana Kane Proctor, author of *Cave of the Casting Bones*

Octogenarian on Fire

New Poems

2013–2017

Vilma Olsvary Ginzberg

McCaa Books • Santa Rosa

McCaa Books
1604 Deer Run
Santa Rosa, CA 95405

Library of Congress Control Number: 2018913031

ISBN 978-0-9996956-7-8

First published in 2018 by McCaa Books,
an imprint of McCaa Publications.

Printed in the United States of America
Set in Tahoma

www.mccaabooks.com

Also by Vilma Olsvary Ginzberg

Poems

Colors of Glass, iUniverse, 2004

Present at the Creation, Ed. with Doug Stout, Small Poetry Press, 2006

Murmurs & Outcries, Small Poetry Press, 2007

Snake Pit, Round Barn Press, 2010

I Don't Know How to Do This, poems on aging, Meridien Pressworks, 2011

making noise, McCaa Books, 2013

90 is the new, McCaa Books, 2018

Octogenarian on Fire, McCaa Books, 2018

Memoir

When the Iris Blooms, 2012

Mostly Roses, 2015

Contents

Introduction and Thanks *8*

1. Writing

the writer's life ***13***

2. Watching the world from here

As a citizen

about necessary evil ***17***
robots ***19***
on canaries and coal mines ***21***
how we got trumped ***23***
to my brother who thinks not as i ***29***
snapshot in Andy Lopez country ***31***
we greens ***32***

As a psychologist

sad is my first name: six haiku ***34***
mothering: a true tale ***36***
padded room ***38***
elegy for the red-breasted bird ***40***
isolation: prisoner ***42***
urban scourge: vampiress verité ***43***
tragic couple: food devolution ***44***
surviving abuse: to see or not to see ***45***

As me

pond scum ***47***
organic gardening, 1930's ***48***
best soup ever ***49***
how to be a hero in these times ***50***
drought ***51***
morning duet ***52***

regeneration ***53***
winter solstice ***54***
four lives, four loves ***55***
cadenza [Rachel Barton Pine] ***65***
silent sky [Henrietta Leavitt] ***66***
were you to please me ***67***
hope ***68***

<u>3. Living in an elding body: challenge and change</u>

life cycle ***71***
being an octogenarian ***72***
good news and bad news: I'm still me ***73***
cranky day ***74***
personal service ***75***
random thoughts on a Tuesday afternoon . . . ***78***
seeing is believing [cataract surgery] ***79***
late afternoon at the DMV ***84***
two views of time ending ***85***
remembering Mom on Mother's Day ***86***
Armstrong redwoods ***87***
downsizing ***88***
moebius of change ***89***
last try ***90***
trauma unit ***92***
    trauma unit 2 . . . . ***93***
    impact ***94***
    trauma nurse ***95***
air: ***1. air hunger*** ***96***
    2. heart failure ***97***
    3. savior ***98***
    4. deliverance ***99***
mirrors and glass ***100***
the unanswerable/the obvious ***101***

About the Author ***103***

Introduction and Thanks

This volume of poems derives from a larger manuscript, titled ***Octogenarian on Fire***, a collection of poetry, memoir and essays written during and about that decade of my life. But it was unwieldy, so I have extracted those poems written in my late eighties, omitted any previously published, and present them on their own here. I plan to produce the balance of that manuscript as part of my memoir series, privately printed for my family.

Writing is one of the main avenues through which I continued to express whatever fire I still possessed, and which was my main preoccupation in those years between 80 and 90: not just writing, but being involved in poet-activist ventures such as the **100Thousand Poets for Change** global peace and justice movement, birthed here in Sonoma County by Michael Rothenberg and Terri Carrion; the **Hurt to Hope** project of the YWCA in which poet Michelle Wing organized writers against domestic violence; and David Madgalene's **World of Change** anthologies of poetry calling for positive social and spiritual change.

Four of my five books of poetry were published after turning 80 [my first was at age 77], as well as two volumes of memoir [family stories written over the years for my granddaughter]. I also served on the board of the Healdsburg Literary Guild for over ten years, hosted its monthly Third Sunday Salon for nine years, produced its annual Poetry Valentine event with chapbook for eight years, and served as its Literary Laureate in 2008/2009. A busy literary ten years indeed!

Simultaneously during that decade I traveled a health odyssey perhaps not so unusual for people of my generation. In addition to a long-held superstition about dying at 83, I experienced a number of health challenges which at times seemed to support that expectation. However, I was surprised by the down- and then up-ward thrust in my overall health; at eighty-eight I was in far better health than I had been five years earlier, and later was able to heal and bounce back remarkably well from a subsequent auto accident injury at age 88. Less than a year later, at 89, after a mentally, emotionally and physically exhausting planned move from my beloved Healdsburg home into the Friends House retirement community in Santa Rosa, I suffered an unexpected episode of congestive heart failure from which I again recovered remarkably well, according to my physicians. As one of the lucky people in this decade of life who experience such recoveries, I include poems that arose from that surprising journey. And for their practical roles in my health challenges, I must thank Dr. Michael Carlston; Dr. John Hunter; Deborah Myers; Greg Bruso , my trainer of over five years; physical therapist extraordinaire David Townsend; and of course Dr. Eki Shola Abrams.

I could not have imagined how this avocation of writing could pull me into a large community of writers and especially poets, many of whom became close friends, most of whom became treasured colleagues. Little did I know until circumstances necessitated it, how generous and supportive so many of this community was. I cannot thank enough, for their friendship, their love, their kindness and generosity, and often their hands-on practical help during my down-times, David Beckman, Waights Taylor, Jerahmy Parsons, Armando Garcia-Davila, Ed Coletti, Katherine Hastings, Jodi Hottel, Toni Wilkes and Greg Randall, David Madgalene, Michelle Wing, Michael Rothenberg and Terri Carrion, Susan Lamont, Liz Martin, Sharon Beckman, and so many others whose caring energies I felt in the hard times and whose common interest in the art and the dissemination of poetry gave me so much joy, always.

And for my non-blood family: music-nighters Geri Cross and Bill Zaner, who saw me through so many ER visits and recoveries; my brother-in-writing Chester Aaron for being constant inspiration; my "chosen daughter" Annelisa MacBean who knows when and how to apply our STAR-knowledge; my dear friends Helen Kincheloe and Mariam Stephens, who hear me; my new sisters-in-writing Clare Morris and Sashana Kane Proctor; to all of them my gratitude for being in my life in such loving, selfless, and soulful ways.

And for my blood family: daughter R-P, granddaughter Rachel, and sister E-A, I feel so lucky to have you in my life, and to feel your loving support and patience for this crazy writing obsession I have.

Then came the devastating Santa Rosa fires of October 2017, nine months after my 90th birthday, giving unexpected poignancy to my title. Another story, that, found in my small impulsive collection, ***90 is the new***.

Sonoma County, California, 2018

1. Writing

Photo by Ann Carranza

Healdsburg Literary Guild

the writer's life

what is the life of the seed
but sitting alone
in some cell of dark

impelled by fire
of unknown origin
to push
to push
somehow
in improvised ways
against boundaries
not of its own making
to leaf
to stretch
to blossom

until
on some air-filled day
        [if graced by good fortune]
all the miracle that had transpired
is plucked
by an innocent
or inquisitive hand

and the seed
finally discovers
its sacred destination

2. Watching the world from here

about necessary evil

what a strange phrase, that:
necessary evil

my mind stretches, pretzels around
to grasp it

what evil could we possibly embrace
because we deem it
necessary

how about weaponry

to teach a man to shoot a gun
is a terrible thing

some said it was a necessary evil
to get food

to send that man to war to kill another man
is a more terrible thing

they said it too was a necessary evil
though I wonder what we got
for that

how about plastic

how about privilege

we insist on remembering why they are necessary
but easily forget why they are evil

that
is the most terrible thing

Photo by Joe Archangelini

World of Change

[Written for the anthology ***World of Change***, David Madgalene, editor, 2014]

robots

when robots clean our rooms
drive our cars
grade our work
trade our stocks
kill our enemies

what is there left
for us to teach our children?

watch "reality" tv fantasies
while downing genetically-modified corn chips
and sodapop
comment on celebs' cleavage
between transformer games
and car chase shows
gripe about potholes
and taxes
show off the latest
and fastest
and clearest
and fullest
and smallest
device full of apps
with which we cannot
pay our keep

and they will
graze as sheep
shop as sheep
vote as sheep
text as sheep
follow and be followed as sheep
each of which believes itself unique
by hashtag

sheep sans wool
sans heart sans soul

robotsheep

Photo by Ann Carranza

100 Thousand Poets for Change

on canaries and coal mines

those pesky wisconsinites are at it again
singing on their lunch hour
in their official public office space
the state capitol rotunda
while their reps are out to lunch
and no legal business being done anyway

they are being arrested
for interrupting the legislative process
of taking away their rights to sing together
peaceably

many white-haired
others young with bodies bent by student loan burden
they are being charged and arrested
handcuffed and booked
for peacefully disrupting
the moneyed invasion by
        the new american fascism
for the lawful assemblage of civilized outrage
        now deemed a danger that must be quelled
for packing no other weapon than
        their alto voices serenading
                we shall overcome

what pesky foolish extremists they are
they need to be put in their place

if they want to sing
they can do it on sundays
in a good christian church
where they can learn to mend their ways
become true god-fearing
real americans
like their governor
that chosen righteous   walker

Introduction to **how we got Trumped**

The ascent of Trump during 2016 left much of the country with jaws agape, and his winning the Electoral College majority threw the entire country for a loop [except for Michael Moore who had predicted his win]. Like many, I was stunned, disappointed, frightened. So I turned to my old faithful companion, writing.

In the following piece, written when he was only a candidate, I try to understand how Trump got as far as he did; intuitively I began with the embracing of television into our daily lives. I also knew that somehow I had to express the dumbed-down mentality that was inherent in its dynamic, in the evolution of our culture, and in the form his rhetoric took.

As a writer I also knew instinctively that I wanted to explore and exploit the similarities between the sparse language of poetry and the simplistic language of mass media, demonstrating by word usage the simplicity of thought that I believe was complicit in the results.

And so I began with our culture's beloved Sesame Street, and wrote this piece in sound-bytes and Madison Avenue-type slogans, attempting to mimic the mind-set I believe contributed to the election of 2016.

It should be read aloud in a fast staccato way so that the listener is carried away without too much chance to think.

how we got Trumped:
[or, how we Americans chose an obscene 1-percenter for POTUS]

let's start here: the next generations and the tube

Sesame Street as baby-sitter: teach by entertaining

cookie monster and big bird

slogans and bytes

short attention span

least common denominator

paragraphs are too hard

don't go now, there's MORE!

We interrupt this news broadcast to bring you...

...to go where you've never gone before...

PBS CNN ABC NBC CBS Fox

TV in every room, every bar, every car, on your phone, on your wrist

TV: first we love it

then we depend on it

then we believe it

keep 'em watching

Mr. Rogers and soap operas and sitcoms

shock and awe and shock-jocks Howard and Geraldo

make it quick

true or false   yes or no   black or white   win or lose

keep me entertained

baseball   football   basketball

right here in my living room

and it's free

Kennedy Nixon debate

Kennedy assassination   Nixon disgrace

history in my living room

just before the crime shows

the only good news is scary news

from interviews of statesmen to politicians on late night

bad attention is better than none

we love our movie stars Reagan Schwartzenegger

rich and famous is better than smart

I wanna be like them

everybody loves a winner

college is for prepping sports stars for wealth

sports   sports   sports

Magic Johnson and Joe Montana and OJ

see it now   live!

winning and earning and selling and earning

famous for being famous

outraged makes it better

Charlie Sheen   Maury Povich   the Kardashians

sex sells

how do I look?

American Idol

vote for your favorite   doesn't matter why

Wall Street : greed is good

mad men ad men

repeat a lie and they'll believe it

QVC   get 'em to buy it

image becomes truth

commercials for information

game shows for quick riches

who doesn't want to be a millionaire?

Oprah Winfrey   Bill Gates   Steve Jobs   Mark Zuckerberg

tragedy sells

drama   disaster   explosions   excitement

nothing is what it seems

is that his real hair/her real boobs/wiener's package?

that's old   what's new?

toilet humor titters

science schmience

my opinion's as good as your facts

Sesame Streeters grown up: entertainment as teacher

no need to read   just watch

OJ   a real star   the real trial   WOW

history on my screen   infotainment

Rush Limbaugh and Bill O'Reilly ....yeah!

tell it like it is

they're famous, they must know

Inside information!   breaking news

send us your cell phone videos

we get it   that's our language

twitters and tweets as news

notoriety as authority

state of the union addresses   ....boooooring......

SNL and Jon Stewart and Bill Maher for the real scoop

the worst thing is boredom

outrageous works every time

Duck Dynasty and white trash

tell it like it is

"reality" shows for excitement

we love the brink of disaster

fear ends within the hour

enter media genius The Donald

anything for attention

ego rules and beauty is required

sex sells and size matters

Miss America   how does she look?

she's only an 8 and too fat

celebrity apprentice

the rich guy that's got it all

he'll show us how

Trump University and the art of the deal

he's the boss

he fires the rich and famous

tweets as facts

forget their minds, grab 'em in the crotch

if you're a star they let you....   Yeah!

celebrity   authority   all the same

the rich are entitled

everybody's gross anyway

whatever

come home dirty and tired

got my beer and football and free TV
I'm tired   I'm mad   I love my guns
I got nothing   I can't lose
How's about a little excitement?
he tells it like it is
yeah we're all equal?
nahhh we ain't
he's just like me with money
I know what he means
8 years a nigger in the White House
now no way a cunt
couldn't be worse than it is now
he knows what I want
I'll follow him   he'll get it done

American Idol   Survivor
Celebrity Apprentice   "You're fired!"
U.S. President   "you're hired!"
all the same he's got my vote
it'll be fixed in an hour
I'll turn it off and go to sleep now

to my brother who thinks not as I

for Dick

decades ago
in our younger freer times
when I lost my own true-blooded brother
and you your sister
I adopted you and you I
we were workmates then
teammates

we locked arms back then
to lift the heavy
clothe the naked
comfort the grieving

we celebrated our victories
with love for each other
mutual respect
and laughter
and harmless teasing for our differences
in sunday morning ritual
and at the voting booth
differences that seemed
trivial then
of small moment
to the caring tasks we shared

these many decades
have parted us
by the many miles
and the tortured bypaths of habit
and shrunk our greetings
into annual report cards
filled with stories of grandchildren grown up
retirement recreations
and loving agreement
to agree to disagree
to omit from our virtual hugs
mention of those inconvenient differences
become chasms

what happened
how could you have slipped
or been slowly swept
to such unfathomable place
how could you
my brother whom I love still
have chosen to stand
on such fetid ground
set your shoulder
to create a suffering world
we once mutually and together
worked to heal

now I mourn not only
for the state of our beloved country
but I pain also
the cost of your understanding
my beloved brother

and I am awash
in the unassailable anguish
the unspeakable sorrow
of the terrible double loss

my dear brother
look again
look down to see
that upon which you stand
should I now fear
the heel of your boot

snapshot in Andy Lopez country*

three Latinos
working at the carwash
polish the newly-soaped-and-rinsed
shiny black and white
police car
its flashers asleep
its motor idle
its stature undeniable

dull shammies
the color of their skin
clear away
all leftover traces
of dutiful vigilance
dust of pursuit
make it new again
ready again
to carry out its mission

protect and serve
it says in the handbook
lying deep in the dark
recesses of the
glove box

* Andy Lopez was a 13-year-old Latino carrying a toy gun, who was shot and killed by a Sonoma County [CA] Deputy. This killing became the focus of a years-long struggle between outraged community members and the supporters of police departments. Repeatedly, 100ThousandPoets held poetry events along with marches and protests over the years. It is still a raw wound locally. This poem was written three years later, when I got a glimpse of a scene at a carwash, where the irony was not lost on me.

we greens

for Michael and Terri

we greens are everywhere
we have been sprouting since life began

broad-leafed or thin
hugging the earth or flying free
        we have been feeding life
air-borne or water-logged
scattering seed or crawling root
close to kin or on our own
        we have been fed by life

whether in clipped and civil pattern
or lawless anarchy
in dense and mottled jungle
or drifting unkind sands
        we persevere

in cracks of craggy rock
on edge of icy floe
in harsh sun's unrelenting glare
        we endure

whether gorgeous and adored
blossoming to accolades
or reviled as weeds
and marked for annihilation
        we persist

we greens
we lively urgent greens
we shyly whispering greens
we pesky insistent greens
many of us native
many more transplanted
        we grow where we are

we greens
we wildly soaring greens
we sharp and prickly greens
        some of us fighting each other for survival
we tendriled clinging greens
we soft and mossy greens
        some of us fighting alone to survive

we all have been transforming light to life
wherever we call home

one clear day
gazing lofty from sequoia land
one or two tall greens
saw the vision wide
dreamed that all that green was one
whispered the message into the ethers
where the winds of change
the breezes of care
carried the call

we are all one
they beckoned
we one hundred thousand
we are the life
we are the grass roots
we cover the earth with the dreams of the people
we are the carriers of life
the reporters of life
the holders of life
the tellers the singers the celebrators of life
we greens
we infinitely varied greens
we who are everywhere
one hundred thousand strong
we are

sad is my first name: six haiku

[for all who have genetic depressive disorders]

sad is my first name
blueprinted in the dendrites
family coat-of-arms

through the lens of blues
first responder to all news
sees but haze-dipped hills

at home with pathos
passion of the Pathetique
sweeps the mourning's floor

sonatas of grief
murmuring in the shadows
lullaby the night

muse of my verses
melding heart to aching heart
melting stone to sand

against such template
pleasures rise in bas relief
jewels for the soul

In my forty years doing psychotherapy in many different settings with many kinds of clients, I learned to distinguish between those conditions which were amenable to psychotherapeutic [non-drug] work, and those which appear to have physical roots in the biochemistry of the brain, such as genetic depressive disorders.

Some of my most rewarding work as a psychotherapist was in intensive residential therapeutic retreats. Though this form of intensive residential therapy is now rarely practiced, it can be powerfully healing for victims of lifelong traumatic personal abuse, as well as social abuse, such as bigotry.

The following pieces are in response to some of those experiences.

The person referred to in the next two pieces happened to be a very large, very angry, middle-aged black man; these attributes were both crucial to, and irrelevant for, the healing with him. After this experience he became an actor who worked for a non-profit dedicated to fostering positive race relations.

mothering: a true tale

for Kevin

1995: workshop in Santa Fe

what draws me to you at this nervous opening session
I'll never know

you: tall sulky
your bent frame too bowed from age alone
mood as dark as your roughly-etched ebony skin
nearly invisible in the light-deprived back row
away from and above the sea of white faces in front
eager for this new adventure
in personal growth

there is something more dire in you
yet despite a danger I know is not mine
I sit beside you
determined to stay
when your body and all it contains
turns even more inward

what a study in contrasts we make:
I with my *saftig* white woman's maturing frame
    wearing carefully-crafted optimism
you decades younger muscled black hulk
    heavy from too much intimacy with darkness
yet underneath the genetic and learned layers
    a pull connection I cannot explain

one by one the newcomers comply
mandatory check-in masks still in place
each mouths strings of words of why they're here
    I've been depressed
    my marriage is falling apart
    I need to find myself
    my therapist thinks this will help
    I hate my job but don't know what to do
    my wife got a lot out of this and thought I would too

some serpent coils tighter in you
I feel my own skin crawl from it

and you, back there, will you let us know who you are
and why you're here?

I sense your knee-jerk reaction to the question
imprisonment in the demand triggers rebellion

I think I'm in the wrong place you mumble
perhaps more to yourself

what do you mean? will you tell us why you decided to come….

now there's a jagged edge to your reply
it was a mistake
I'm the only person of color here
this is not the place for me

I know you mean it   think what's here is not for you
serpent coiled even tighter
I know you just want to leave   escape this same old shit

a flurry of demurs from the group
slides off your toughened skin
you have heard too many empty welcomes
sheathing shivs of fear, hatred, rejection

until the fair-skinned ginger-haired southern delicacy
delivers that sweet and lethal hemlock
some of my best friends …….

group leader's valiant attempt at antidote
rubs it even deeper into that rewounded place
where the serpent prepares to strike
you alone its target

I bow my head with yours
hear myself whisper *soto voce* to you alone
but with the urgency of adrenalin
god I hate that almost as much as you do
but you gonna let that stupidity rob you?
if you play the race card as excuse to leave
you'll miss out on what you came here to find
and you'd be a bigger fool than I thought

I sit fast…heart pounding…waiting…knowing I'm right
hoping you know too

padded room

mattresses cushion the floor and walls
of this windowless sweaty little room
filled with massive mounds of pillows
wire cage over the single ceiling light
the most sacred place I know

I sit cross-legged in the corner
hand you the red plastic bat
invite you to let loose

coiled serpent roused
by remembrance of childhood horrors
        humiliations   deprivations
you are terrorized by your own rage
chained by decades of restraint
forced by fear   and mother's practiced civility
        that kept you all alive
you cannot now let go   it is too dangerous

I know what is under that rage
        and under that
                and under that
and I am not afraid
        I'm here for you I say *and I'm not leaving you*
        and pray you believe it

serpent makes careful trial pass
no venom there
        I am not afraid of your rage I say
        how long will you hold on to it?
        leave it in this room I say   *I will stay with you*

while I watch you risk   and finally let loose
I silently cheer your courage
marvel at your endurance   past and present
        powerhouse of fury released   then fear   then shame
                watch you shed lifetimes of pain

hours later you fall exhausted into my arms
I rock you like a child and weep for all your unearned wounds
        I'm so sorry   I'm so sorry
I speak for myself and all my fellow perpetrators

Kevin, after 1995

elegy for the red-breasted bird

for Robin Williams

red-breasted bird
crimson song as wide as his heart
gifts of joy flying off every feather
bringer of light and promise
that dark and cold are not forever

to exorcise his pain
he has taken his all from us

to end the despair
he has bled his wounds to silence

hearing again the mourning-shrouded message
that something was at its end
its time was up
he thought it meant his life entire

all too common a mistake

the hand of death abides
holds the hand of life itself
they walk together yin and yang through all our days
our battles   our celebrations   our silent hours

we who tire of the unwelcome darkness
we who cannot imagine
coming through the next endless night
we who hear the roaring siren call of surcease
and lie in the shadows of forgetting
are easy prey for the lurking error

the knife is always at the ready
it can kill   or it can pare

behold how often do we prune the vine so it will flower
dead-head the rose to urge its blossom
run one more lap to tone the tired muscle

it is too late for him
red-breast will not serenade again

but the call to die will rise in us again
the call to death is real   its urgency intense
demanding response it will not disappear

but let us listen again
it is a gift   a priceless tune
and we must remember how to hear it

we must harken   we must seek
we must embark on the dark treasure hunt

until the hidden culprit is known
until what must be heard behind the siren-song is heard
until what has become burden is left behind
until what keeps us fettered is released
until that which is at its end is allowed to die

so that all that can still live and laugh and love in us
does remain

R I P

isolation: prisoner

on this over-crowded spinning globe
over-run by frantic-shrouded apathy

there is a loneliness of journey
that cannot be assuaged
by tweet or twitter
by crowded coliseum of sport
by endless assault of commerce

there is a silence that resides
in secret caves of endless night
that cannot be reached
by love-intentioned reassurance
or best-paid advice
not even the tithed divine

it is both fearsome nightmare
and unsolicited gift

as fearsome nightmare
it explodes in columbine and newtown
oakland and ferguson

as unsolicited gift
I am helpless in its tight hold
until these words
break me free

urban scourge: vampiress *verité*

[written after a three-year battle with bedbugs]

ancient blood-sucker of the ages
unstoppable
forever thirsty for that warm and sticky feast

creature of the night
silent
mistress of stealth
shunning light of day
of candle
of logfire

prey of none
fearless by birth
predator of license

under cover of somnus
does she go about her nightly rounds
until sated
full
appeased
in silence does she scurry back
to her secret nest
to populate the shadows
with her kind
takers all
givers of naught
but misery

by what divine mistake
what joke of evolution
what meanness of cosmic spirit
is she in our midst

we need no dracula
no twilight fantasy

beware
you will not like
the vampiress *verité*

tragic couple: food devolution

he liked to eat
she liked to dine

he married her for her class
she thought she'd show him how

she couldn't
so she joined him
eating

he thought she got frumpy
lost her polish

disappointed
he started scarfing his food
before the tv set

feeling like a failure
she gave up eating
started cutting her wrists in the kitchen
instead

their friends and family wonder
why they never go to restaurants any more
what happened to their mutual love
of food

surviving abuse: to see or not to see

[inspired by, and dedicated to, all those powerless young girls on the planet who are considered property of men who use them so]

close your eyes 'til it's over, girl
ain't always such a mess
close your eyes 'til it's over, girl
won't make you any less

close your eyes 'til it's over, girl
's a better world inside
close your eyes 'til it's over, girl
ain't never sin to hide

close your eyes 'til it's over, girl
this pain will soon be done
jes close your eyes 'til it's over, girl
til the need to live is won

close your eyes 'til it's over, girl
jes close your eyes real tight
that world inside will keep you safe
until the mornin's light

close your eyes
and pray real hard
'til it's over, girl
'til it's over, girl

then open 'em up and come on out
there's another world out here
open 'em wide
come on outside
we been there
                    we're here
                                        we're here.....

....and now a shift to some gratitudes.........

My Healdsburg pond and waterfall

pond scum

my fish pond has sprung a leak
leaving water lilies high and dry,
fish struggling in shallow murk

I skim off pond water into tub
temporarily house fish there
and ponder the murky bottom:

inside soft silky folds of muddy mystery
primordial slime teases its secrets
hides promise of genesis power

brown-green murky mystery
slides through my curious fingers
yielding miniscule miracles:

sometime fish, surviving or suffocated,
mud-enveloped larval creatures,
fry, snail, algae, cell

pond scum womb of us all
this original eden suddenly sacred
calls me back to some nameless beginning

earthwater that gives life
earthwater that takes life

this home of the eater and the eaten
whispers siren-song to sister cells
in my own wordless caves

organic gardening, 1930s

back then
everybody with a plot of ground
or a backyard
had an old gnarled fruit tree
or brambled berry bushes
yielding buckets of juiciness
in exchange for thorn-scratches
or a pathetic though much-tended grapevine
even in New Jersey

the hardware store carried
nuts and bolts and rakes
but no pesticides
sold by a man
with hoe-toughened hands

when the apple we picked to eat
had a small black borehole
and a worm in the core
my Dad used to say

that one's a good apple
it's been tested and it passed
look at all the good apple
he left for you
thank him
and eat around him
and then throw him back
under the tree
to his family

best soup ever

for my music night friends

skin and bones of thanksgiving turkey
bearing shreds of tasty flesh
swathed in gratitude
simmered to their marrow
until they yield their very essence
to the rich golden broth

verifiable vegetables *veritas*
bathed in adoration
groomed, peeled, chopped, sliced, diced
the old-fashioned way
by hand as they say
before being sent in holy sacrifice
into the cauldron

handfuls of garden greens kept frozen
just for this
scattered like confetti
eau de herbes
pinch of cumin dash of coriander
gild of turmeric crush of clove
juice of lemon
oh the aromas

oodles of noodles
and there you have it

a feast for the palate
a treat for the nose
a gift for friends
a ritual of celebration
a missile of love

how to be a hero in these times

If you don't want to wear silly spandex costumes, learn to fly, weave spider webs, strike down enemies with lasers, or be in the limelight, but you still would like to be a hero here on Planet Earth, here's what to do:

1) take up the study of beekeeping,

2) keep bees,

3) learn all you need to, to help increase the health and number of bees,

4) make what you've learned available to all who would follow suit,

5) be prepared to be busy as a bee.

If you like, you can do this hero work quietly and anonymously. You will still be a hero. There are some few who already are.

drought

drought-ravaged earth
its crust thick with thirst
sloughs off the meager trickle
as if it has forgotten how to drink
how to hold the moist'ning waters
on its parched tongue

unyielding now
it clenches deep the roots
themselves tunneling
burrowing
in singular search
for any buried sustenance

cracks and furrows
hug the dusty seeds
in holy desperation
the hope of all nature's embraces:
wait for a teardrop of relief
and make another generation
if you can

morning duet

grey dove
flutters soft her long and slender wings
finds perch on thinning branch
just beyond my shoulder left

poised on twiglet low
croons she her mournful morning dirge
into my ear
insisting that
I hear
I hear
her sorrow's song
the end is near
the end is near

I fault her not
it is her charge
to so display her melody

just as it is mine
to place the tender seed
into the cradling earth
with my unspoken tune
there is no end
to seedlings sown
to seedlings sown

regeneration

tiny branchlet broken off its mother plant
rescued from the unkind parched earth
its thirsty wounded limb
plunged into the tiny blue vase
put on a windowsill
to survive if it can

today
after a northern winter's wait
two thin pristine white rootlet strings
sinew from the crook of stem and leaf
down into the dying life-giving water
desperate thrusts for life
oblivious of fate
cosmic natural or human
seeking nothing but to live
on the delicate point of now

I serve you tea
and memories from before you
plunging them into
the life-giving blue vase
of who you are
pristine white strings
sinew down my core
through the dying life-giving waters
oblivious of fate
human natural or cosmic
wanting nothing but to celebrate
the delicate living point of
now

winter solstice

days, wearing their dark cloaks
floor-length
slink quietly from dusk to dusk
leaving our spirits heavy-lidded
our souls light-hungry

across the shadowed globe
throughout the eons
we have gathered in dimmed rooms
creating desperate festivals

wrapping our caves our dreams
with strings of light-shards

lighting banks of candles

snuggling before flames
of family and friend and hearth

reading from ancient promises

drinking fire to warm the thinning blood

singing
chanting
recounting
supplicating
forgiving
planning renewals

sparking up our foggy hopes
for light-abundance

and license to squander it
when it returns

four lives, four loves

it is time to talk about love
or more accurately
time to talk about my loves

one

I have had four loves in my lifetime
if I count that first passionately painful
dazzlement at fourteen
that private obsession
with the high school football player
whom every girl in the building adored
every girl
each of whom wanted
with the same drive he ran the ball
to be on his arm for the prom

we touched but once
hips side by side in a small car
crammed with truant students
he lifted his pigskin arm
over my head
his fingers lighting
on my far shoulder
I would have consented
to die ecstatic
had I been asked

but who was I
shy and shrinking as I was
nerdish A- student that I was
sans make-up bare-faced
non-fashionista in my poor plain drabs
buried in my books
who was I
to even dare dream
dare dream even
to be on such a handsome hero's arm

who did I think I was
head bowed
to hard work at school
to survival labor at home
to class consciousness on the street

you have to raise your eyes to dream
who was I to even dream
except perhaps at night
under cover
under covers
at fourteen

. . . .

at least
that clumsy awakening
of my young hormones
was far from rare
unlike the later loves
which were
nevertheless
of great moment

two

I was twenty-five
and there HE was
older than my parents
smart so smart no
really educated knowing so much
about so much
well-travelled   cultured
admired respected dignified
mature   honorable
funneling all he knew
through his embracing world view
his faulty heart
failing too soon

generous of time of spirit
intolerant only of intolerance
he loved the imperfect world
he loved his challenging work
he loved those he cared for
he loved them beyond their pain
their struggles
loved them to health
left healing in his wake

until one impossible day
he told me he loved me
me
ignorant apprentice
dazzled follower
grateful sponge of his light
me
how could he
he
love
me   me
a nobody to his stature

though others might have wondered
if he were of flawed heart
and foolish mind
or flawed mind and foolish heart

he was neither
and I
disbelieving
nevertheless accepted

I was to learn later
he confessed his love for me
not to me first
but first to his first wife
who was mentor to me
his loyal life-time companion
his savior heart mender
peers were they
equal in history language wisdom
both wide and personal

and she
she
asked his desire
which was he said
to spend the rest of his few-numbered days
with me
if I would have him
and she
in her long-practiced love
counseled
why don't you ask her?

and so he did
and so was I dumb-founded
on that impossible day
when I was hit
with love in multiple forms

without much thought
I agreed
overwhelmed by compliment
such as I never believed I could deserve
to be gifted by such a woman
of such unselfish generosity
to be loved by such a man
of such great character
to be wanted by such a man
was beyond belief beyond dream

and so
out of her boundless quiet love
she released him
without condition   open-handed
without regret   open-hearted
as she always was

in bedazzled blindness
did I walk with him
while he insisted I be
not in his shadow

in time
bathed in his respect for me
basking in his honesty with me
I felt his love for me
under my skin
lost my barriers to his
integrity his
wholeness
was pulled up
out of my mud of ego
by his light
into my own blossoming
began to see in myself
that which he had first seen
under the dross
that shone with promise
that that he loved

came to love him
as true wife
consummation careful warm mature
learned to love him anew
as mother   co-parent of his first child
my first child my only child
our only child
as co-creator of our works
protected the progeny of his fertile mind
dressed his words
scattered seeds of his ideas
carefully fed his weakening heart

tended him
when that stumbling heart
finally laid him low
when he was but sixty

at the end
held his colding hand
on his last bed
promised to take care
of his precious pearl daughter
loved him with a love unequaled
loved him with the love of decades
after only three years and some

was left a grieving
and grown-up widow
at twenty-nine

three

throughout those following urbane years
of my prime
among all the others
enjoyed for passing pleasures

this one stood apart

his openness beguiling
his candidness seductive
his lightness open to interpretation
unexpected adventure
sparking from his
pastoral eyes

I was reading why not now
in his beckoning smile
let's go
in his lithe limbs

daring me not
guileless   carefree
he merely invited
and I went
throwing to the winds
all I'd become

our times together
mardi gras festivals
breaks from our separate
office-wrapped lives
kept as discrete
as safe-held treasures

we'd meet for weekend getaways
harleying vacation highways
toward hidden sanctuaries
to sleep like furred or naked creatures
howling   laughing   under unblinking stars
flying to realms newly known
exploring image and skin
palate and verse
underworld and overtone

he upended me
willing cohort
out of my earned repute
rumbled open my
sleeping lava flows
our consummations careless
pubescent   fiery

reckless adolescents were we
escaped from our daily desks
challenging the world to find us
toss us about
spit us happily out

I loved him with the abandon
of a wild first love

~~~I sometimes marvel
in hindsight, how we ever
sideswiped catastrophe
heedless as we were
whether my second love
protected me from somewhere
letting me call it
luck~~~
~~~

but in time my root-hungriness
like banyan tree
reached to tentacle this
wild freedom-loving
serial sampler
if not to me
beside me

while I yearned to aching
for the solace of routine
he would not be manacled so

his thirst for the next new
unassuaged
he slipped away
as if for just another day

and stayed away

and stayed away

away   a place I could not share

away became years of tears
in slow silent swirl with eons of ennui

until memories
losing their luster
like yesterday's confetti
were swept
muddied
bloodied
under the rug
of never-was

he was my wild and perilous love
that fiery four years
carnival ride
of my youthful teens
which he brought delayed
into my orbit
when we were
all of
forty-two

four

this is how it is when, in your eighties
the perfect love of your 23rd year dreams
like in youth and temper
dark-eyed   lithe   open-hearted   romantic
loving   lovely
suddenly appears
wraps his luminous words
around your longing

this is how it is

containing all the ages I've ever been
that 23-year-old I was/am
bright   hopeful   ripe   luscious
has jumped alive full-bodied
resurrected
into my now thrombosing heart

there are no words
for the sheepish shame I feel
when her excitement escapes

there are no words
for the senseless cruelty
of the time warp

there are no words
for the aching hunger
for what never was
and now can never be

there are no words
for the bitterness
crawling on my wrinkling skin

curled on my lonely couch
sparse the words
for the threadbare throw of gratitude
that barely warms but cannot quite
comfort me
as I drink his poesy of revelation
remembering what never was

this is how it is when, in your eighties
the perfect love of your 23rd year dreams   appears

***cadenza**: In concerti the term *cadenza* often refers to a portion of a concerto in which the orchestra stops playing, leaving the soloist to play alone in free time

From Wikepedia: On January 16, 1995, Pine was severely injured in a train accident in the suburb of Winnetka, where she taught violin lessons. As she was exiting a Metra commuter train with her violin over her shoulder, the doors closed on the strap to her case, pinning her left shoulder to the train. The doors, which were controlled remotely and had no safety sensors, failed to reopen, and she was dragged 366 feet by the train before being pulled underneath and run over, severing one leg and mangling the other. Pine was saved by the prompt application of tourniquets by several passengers who disembarked from the train after pulling its emergency brake handles. She sued Metra and Chicago NorthWestern Railroad for compensation for her injuries and legal and medical expenses. Metra argued that she made the choice not to extricate her arm from the strap of the violin case due to the value of the instrument, a 400-year-old Amati valued at around $500,000, and thus she carried most of the blame for her injuries. The jury ruled in Pine's favor. Metra changed its conductor safety procedures following the incident and made other changes to the trains themselves.

Rachel Barton Pine

cadenza*

for Rachel Barton Pine

from out of the jaws of inconsiderate
fate
from out of the caverns of subterranean pain
you consoled your confusions
        with the melodies of genius
improvised your coda-ed questions
until the answers growled your presence
        back into the concert halls
where now
standing aloft on man-made legs
you whisper your perturbations
until they are pulled fine and tender
        on thin Guarneri strings
        into the ether of our dreams
insist your passion into the classrooms
        your gratitude into the rehab halls
carol your crescendos
across the shadowed valleys
        to glisten the mountaintops
sweeten the innocent moon

the shatter of biting steel
scattered like stars
turned to cosmic joy

silent sky

for deaf astronomer Henrietta Leavitt

around silent sky
planets twirl in ceaseless dance
asteroids abscond

above silent sky
stars gleam their ardent love songs
moon bursts into bloom

beneath silent sky
trillium nods in deep wood
cricket stops his song

beside silent sky
I slumber in dreamless dawn
nudged awake too soon

were you to please me

bring me no candy bring me no wine
bring me no jewels shiny or fine

bring me instead

an oval of avocado
softly sweet as a baby's lips

a tree of broccoli
strong and green as the life it gives

a flask of fine EVOO
smoothing balm of the appetite

a chunk of chocolate
dark and rich as the soothing night

honey from the nearest bee
salve for the soul's thanks-giving

a poem or two or even three
from this sacred life you're living

hope

hope is those grandmothers who an hour ago
each donned their black slacks and black tops
to stand together on the corner
something they've done at noon every Friday for the last ten years
joining other women in black
across the country across the seas across all boundaries
in that grief that silent blade of protest
against their sons' seduction into the glories of war

hope is the loan-battered college senior
and the corporate-battered retired senior
singing together we shall overcome
in the madison rotunda
before being arrested for disturbing the peace they bring
singing tall into their captors' faces

hope is the music clanged out by the unwashed the untaught
who never heard of Mozart
but who beat out their dreams on the garbage can lids
of their lost and listless tenement neighborhoods
hanging rhythm on the clotheslines
hip-hop of a new journey out of the cracked cement

hope is the gathering of elding beatniks and limping Viet vets
and tattooed gen-X-ers and loud lipsticked goths in a coffee house
reading poems of protest peace and solidarity
to the beat of a bass viol's plaintive heart

hope is a Masai daughter on her knees
planting sprouts in the dusty clay of a savannah plain
or the soft earth of a white house garden
teaching the children that love sits on the tongue of the nourished

hope sprouts from the fingers of anyone who ever plants a tree

hope may sleep out of reach for a while but never dies
you may kiss it awake any time

3. Living in an elding body: challenge and change

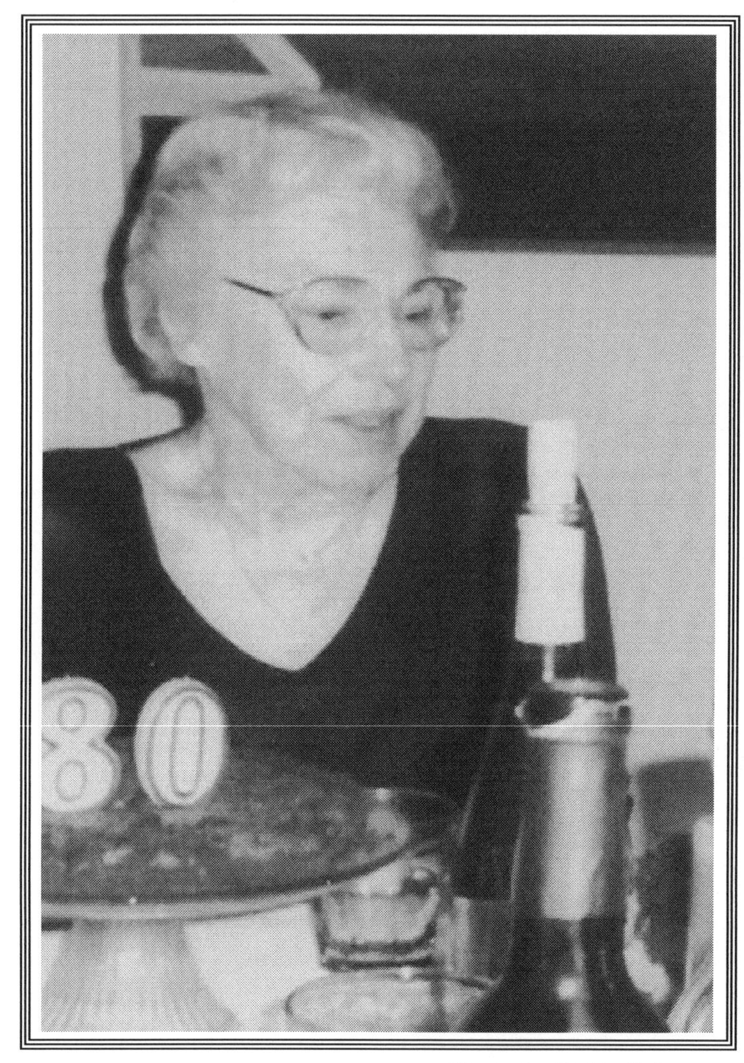

Photo by Batja Cates

Turning 80
January 17, 2007

life cycle

[written at age 79...an unintended prophecy]

childhood is hell
I'm glad I never had one
who would want a life
of aimless enjoyment
and narcissist indulgence
at that tender an age?

born grown-up I was destined
to be helper protector
responsible caretaker
did my job well
teachers loved me

good thing my adolescence was postponed
until my feisty forties
so much better to live
that free and dangerous time
in the rock-solid middle years

this seemingly out-of-sync sequence
has granted me
the best gift of all:
my eighties promise to be
my prime

driving force

[written on my 80th birthday]

I'm in the fast lane at 80 ----
this is no time to doze off!

Being an octogenarian

When mirrors still lie but pictures don't

When nothing new for your wardrobe is right any more

When you can't understand how college kids don't know what FDR did

When everything, absolutely everything, takes longer to do

When it hurts to chew lettuce

When they don't ask any more whether it's a senior ticket you want

When you're counting steps per day instead of miles

When people tell you how great you look

When you're lucky to get one friend over for dinner and you have all those service for eight sets

When now seems so endless and later so short

When you can't answer any of the pop culture questions on Jeopardy

When your wisest understandings happen when no one's around

When no one's around a lot these days

When your hearing is good but you can't get the lyrics any more

When you're delighted to be talking to that interesting young man until you see yourselves in the mirror

When your AARP kids are deciding whether to take early retirement or not

When too often for comfort you can't help but wonder how and when it will happen

good news and bad news: I'm still me

the good news when I was younger: my blood pressure was low
the bad news: when I stood up fast I was light-headed

now that I'm old[er] the good news is: my blood pressure is still low
the bad news: I can't get up that fast any more

but, hey, the bad news is: a lot of people my age are dead
the good news: I ain't

I know I'm older
but I'm still the same me

I'm still dependable
but maybe a little more slowly so

I'm still independent
but maybe a little more carefully so

I'm still generous
but maybe a little more wisely so

I'm still outspoken
and maybe a little more loudly so

cranky day

today is one of those days
today I'm cranky

today I'm cranky at my laundry
which drops undisciplined
one sock at a time
on my way to the washer

today I'm cranky at my breakfast dishes
that haven't washed their own faces
and stacked themselves neatly
by lunch-time

today I'm cranky at my favorite old shoes
that are wearing out
faster than I am
how dare they

today I'm cranky at the junk mail
and the spam email
and the gas company that insists
its smartmeter on me
unless I pay them extra
to keep the old one
does that make sense or am I crazy too?

today I'm really cranky

not a good day
to call in that favor
remind me my taxes are due
break the last shoelace

but maybe it's a good day to
discover the baby rosebud
in my garden
the special azure
of today's windless sky
the way the mockingbird can still catch my breath
and sing it to the world

personal service

expecting someone more anonymous-looking
I enter into this encounter with this stranger
awkwardly
noticing his youth his beautiful but guarded
eyes   his shy smile

our clumsiness of talk
        or what passes for it
really only faint sounds or nods
hardly any eye contact
barest minimum needed to come to agreement
passes awkwardly between us
as I begin taking off the appropriate coverings

though well along in years I am new
to this pedicure thing
unclothing parts of myself
reawakens memories of earlier first barings
and I am again a-stutter and inept

when I try to help him roll up my slack's legs
for easier access to my bare feet my ankles my calves
he gently brushes me off
taking over the job
leaving me little choice but to relax
into the receptiveness I had yearned for in anticipation
yet now find strangely discomforting

proceeding with his task of providing this
personal service
he displays his familiarity with this anatomy
his excellence of skill
while I
unaccustomed as I am
play customer
try to exude a certain minimum jadedness
a coolth I am not feeling
as if having a stranger touch my bare skin
in such a private way
is as everyday for me
as   breathing

he is gentle with the lotions
slow of stroke
skilled fingers finding their mark easily
as he carefully lifts out or sets back my feet
into the just-right warm bubbling water
    one at a time
massages my toes
    one by one
trims the nails
    one by careful one
pats my skin dry with tender towels
rubs the circulation back into my tired ankles
    one by delicious one

watching him do his artful thing
I wonder where his mind is now
wanting to believe it is with me
but guessing it is not
even while he glances up every so often
to see if he is doing it all for my liking
and I smile only slightly to keep it
    impersonal
this thing between us that feels so
        intimate

should I just close my eyes
let myself go
like the young woman in the next chair
who moans in half-whisper
as the middle-aged woman at her feet
tends similarly to her

does he care
as his perfect hands on my bare skin imply
or
has he done this a million times
and I am just one of the many

I am embarrassed that I even wonder so

as he continues in his unhurried way
his beautiful Mona Lisa face giving me no clue
I gradually almost unwillingly

settle into the pleasure
but only
after some subtle and invisible wall
erects itself silently inside me

after long last
in an unnatural understanding
I know this intimacy with this stranger
unlike other intimacies I have known
must end now no strings attached
no expectations   no future
each of us taking from it what we need
I this temporary gateway to a fantasyland of care
he
I know not what other than the money

my feet still tingling warm
I fumblingly pay at the counter for the service
leaving him a tip

and think of coming again
vowing to be more clear next time
about how real and how pretend
this all is
this hands-on intimacy with a stranger
in a public place
these impersonally-delivered acts
so intimately satisfying
this personal service so jarringly commercial

and suddenly I know
in a jolt of understanding
something about
the johns I always hated

random thoughts on a Tuesday afternoon

most people my age are dead
I want more being alive while I'm alive

preferring to live at home instead of in a home
paying for a personal trainer to keep me on my feet

new roof or new teeth?

thankful for native plants, hummingbirds, and bees

inching up the Tylenol doses as more joints creak in one by one

my friends are too ill to come over or too ill to have me come over
some people would give an arm to have as much solitude as I have

my doctor wants me to update my final wishes
I'm too young to have final wishes
don't want to be too old for new wishes

glad the things I must cook to mush are things I like

the internet questionnaire says I can expect to live to 103
my financial advisor says her tables say 97
who fills in those *whoops!*?

haven't baked cookies in decades
can't throw away the cookie cutters

living alone and loving it hating it treasuring it fearing it
write when I feel like it
afraid of choking, every day
love those days all day in my robe

just in style neglecting my drought-wrought garden
wrote saving water on my dusty car

while the rosebushes dry up, blossom no more
I drink water and read the papers
avoiding premature death at 87

at least I don't have a houseful of cats like some old ladies

seeing is believing [cataract surgery]

for Dr. Gary Barth

One

these marbles of magic
these marvels of magic
these orbs set in perfect balance
beneath our brows
swallowing light in measured doses
plumbing the shadows
finding the way

just one of the many things that change unnoticed with the years

the dimming comes slowly
silently over time
the shy softening
the quiet smoothing of harsh lines
the guazy glow of my mirrored face
the pride I take in my smooth skin
the sunniness of it all
confirming the myth of golden years

it is the scattering of the light
like Van Gogh's starry nights
like his haloed poolroom pendants
swirled and surrounded
        that gives me pause
daytime sunbeams glaring
nighttime headlights blinding
        that give me pause

creeping muddy-ochred glare
hiding all behind it
every window ... and none ... awash
with the cruel blur of kindness
like the vaselined lenses glorying aging stars' visages
the glamour the ego
        also give me pause ... I wait ...

Two

the time comes, as it always does
when no valorous squint
no corrective lens
can undo the roiling muddiness growing within
and the fearsome knife so long resisted
becomes the only choice

piece of cake they all say
no problem
get it done
you'll be so glad

Three

the appointments to prepare
the agreements to confirm
the forms to fill
        and sign
the drops to take
the night-time imaginings
the reflexive blinking
        just thinking
they say 97% success
I don't want to be
        in the other three
can I turn back now
would it be wisdom
        or cowardice
and yet
it gets worse not better
so I'd better

Four

it's outpatient surgery
the waiting room with my driver friend
more forms   is there no end to the forms
too long a nervous while
trying not to be
by chatting
or feigning comfort in the silences

finally the invitation into the prep room
as if it were for tea
the cheery nurses
in their choreography
one puts me on the gurney
pillows me in comfort
another bracelets my wrist
marks which eye and puts drops into it
another a needle in my vein
another a blanket on my feet
I ask each her name and memorize them
they say I will be awake but feel no pain
are you OK they ask
I don't know what OK is
but always say yes
don't want to seem dumb
or out of it

lots of alone times in between
lots of listening to the same riffs
with the curtained others also being prepped
it is and is not an assembly line

surgeon in his blue scrubs
quick scan of the clipboard
a personal question or two
anesthetist the same
I am over-answering
more like cocktails than tea
I can't seem to stop
words tumbling from my mouth
as if they were my last
to be spoken now or forever lost

I am rolled into the operating room
strangely unafraid
noticing details too numerous to tell
white ceiling
bright lights
blue-clad people on the outside edges
they ask   I answer
when they are silent I hear myself chatter

I know he is at my eye
though I feel nothing
but oh! ... the light show!
blotting out the ceiling
brilliant circles of blue and red and green
and large white flashes
so clear the hues so bright the edges
so many shapes
dancing around each other
in joyous celebration
I and only I can see it
my very own and mine alone
all inside my very head
I love this light show I say
over and over
and wonder why
nobody ever told me this part

they roll me out
is it over already?
I loved the light show
and soon I am sitting comfy
in the little coffee break corner
my friend beside me
orange juice and blueberry muffins
the cheery nurses in their choreography
checking in
you did fine
make sure you wear the dark glasses
and call day or night
if you feel any pain

<u>Five</u>

riding home unaccustomed in the passenger seat
unaccustomed to the light
even with the dark glasses
the luxury of just looking around oh my!
reading signs before passing them oh my!
carnival colors all abound
no one can tell I'm just minutes post-op
not even me

Six

a quick brothy soup when we get home
home
a place I see anew
I don't remember those colors on the wall
but especially the whites
I can't believe the whites
how blue and clear they are
white
not ivory-white but blue-white
bright white
white white
white full of light
a radiant white fridge to open
pristine pendant illuminates the kitchen counter
virginal scratch-pads waiting for their first notes
light in the white corners of the bath
the real age of my well-lined face
fool's paradise replaced by wonder

in the next hours   days
even weeks
I re-discover the blue in everything
the hue the yellow mist had made impotent
has returned in all its strident glory
the multitude of blues in my closet
I had thought were one
now uncovered   separated   rediscovered
blue jeans and navy slacks
blue states
cerulean sky and cobalt bottles
azure eyes of babies and indigo shadows of eve
the blue that makes my favorite magenta sweater
        art-worthy brilliant
the rich royalty of plum and grape
the cheer of lavender and passion pink
scarlet   crimson   ruby   cherry
all re-aflame like me

at 87 I have the wide eyes
of a child newly seeing

late afternoon at the DMV

To the DMV clerk at window 23
who served me today at the end of her day
after I'd waited two hours:

I'm sorry you had a mean grandmother
or maybe she was sick.....alzheimer's?

but anyway......I'm not her

and I'm sorry if my recent cataract surgery has not yet
fully healed and I fumbled for my pen because none of my
glasses work any more and it's too early for the new ones and
that's why I'm here to postpone my driver's test
as my surgeon suggested

and I asked about those three questions on the form
just before you got testy

I do this only once every few years
but I imagine as your everyday job it must get really tiresome
so many different people to deal with
and some of them might really ask dumb questions

but how are you to know that even though I'm grey and wrinkly
my education is holding up pretty well
and my fumbling is not about senility
or whatever made you impatient with that
grandmother I remind you of.....or was it your mom

or is it the chintzy paycheck you probably get
you look like you could do way better than this
three-by-three carrel squeezed in

or that this is a bad flu year and you never know....
all those people...... waiting
waiting with their coughing
waiting with their crying babies
waiting with their numbers
for the automated voice to say

G148 you will be served at window 23

two views of time ending

I wake from a dream
where the hour hand of my clock
rushes by like seconds
as I risk missing
the distant departing plane

I take my waking refuge in my garden
under the trees where the crisp
pumpkiny leaves of fall
fall as if they have hours to drift

time has become more elastic than ever
days embraced by joy shrink too soon
into specters of shaky remembrance
while hours of mindless emptiness stretch
beyond where the grieving heart
can give them life
or erase their reach

I cannot hurry any more

neither dare I waste time any more

I am caught between
the racing clock
and the immense exhaustion
of this faltering flesh

Lonely
and shining moments with you
no longer stand aloft
sun-tipped mountain-tops
forever gracing the landscape
of my days
but are eroded at their feet
by the dark mire
of too many unremarkable days
slowly marching my life away

Grateful
while yet the dark mire
of too many unremarkable days
softly march my life away
stay yet a while
shining moments with you
stand aloft
sun-tipped mountain-tops
forever gracing the landscape
of my life

remembering Mom on Mother's Day

they appear unbidden in my inbox:
poems for Mother's Day

Billy Collins' *Lanyard,*
about the useless thing he hand-made for her as a child

Rafael Jesus Gonzalez' *Mother's Day 2015*
about the blankets she hand-made that warmed him

I call my last surviving sib
my octogenarian sister a continent's width away
just in, she says, from basking outside
for her daily dose of D
and I read their poems to her

we talk about Mom
her early-onset arthritis and persistent resourcefulness

how she held sway against her parents
for love of our Dad
whose vulnerable frailties gave her
so much private grief and public shame

how she survived the Great Depression
single-handedly for our family

how she made do   and taught us how

how we are like her and how we are different
how we felt about it back then
how we feel about it now

how our pitiful gifts of clay ashtrays for her
...Mom hated Dad's smoking...
mirrored Collins' camp-braided lanyard

how her life-long output of crocheted afghans
therapy for her arthritis-gnarled hands
mimicked the knitted blankets of Gonzalez' Mom's
her life-force transcending the niche's urn
bright stitches warming us still

Armstrong redwoods

oldest living thing on earth
ancient redwoods
dressed in early morning fog
standing tall   wise
giant wordless witness
to trillium dripping morning dew
fern weeping into dry creek bed

ancient families gather
in tight circles of tribute
around mothers fallen
suck at her roots
breathe her history
meditate in gratitude

under the craggy bark
the only truth
eons of time layering

under my skin
the craggy truth

downsizing

today I am cleaning out file drawers
discarding mountains of paper

letters of reference
certifications
licensing
office notes and memos
annual reports
thank you notes from grateful clients

lab reports
my doctor's hand-written note
with the bad news
referrals to specialists
health records copies
post-surgery instructions

get-well cards and
happy birthday cards and
welcome to your new home cards and
thinking of you cards and
old phone numbers and
concert programs and
volunteer schedules and
IOU's

too many final goodbyes
yielded to the shredder

the deaths are a million
paper cuts drawing blood
reminding me how alive
have been my years
all the breath-ful minutes

moebius of change

surrounded by that I love
I am pre-wrapped
in its absence
I will not walk this beloved path again
the chill
fills the changing air

all I now assume
will no longer be
I am filled with love for
what I have still
and miss already

I grieve
even before I leave

though it is the road I choose
I weep for what I
am about to lose

the not yet gone
heavy with its
disappearance-to-come
shines bright in my eyes
sheds sweet and salty tears

weep not
whispers the smooth surface
the twisted consolation

it is better I meet tomorrow
light and ready
cleansed by today's premature
but love-filled
sorrow

last try

it was the fineness of his flailing
which first caught my eye
those barely noticeable motions
and then
the fact that he was on his back
a position not, I guessed, taken for sport
that held my curiosity

larger than fly, not bee, finer-bodied than wasp
some winged six-legged cousin
clearly in distress
legs reaching sideways or akimbo
grabbing at the concrete surface under him
struggling to right himself
he slides in sideways circles on his back instead

looking closer
I see his hind left leg dragging
not just useless to lift him in one direction
or support him in the other
but now an obstacle

just out of his reach lay a dry shred of leaf
playing breeze, I move it closer to him
a casual life buoy meant to help him save himself

though he struggles
it does not help him to his feet

now on the inescapable path of rescue
I offer him, more deliberately, the shard of leaf
his long bent stick-legs grab it
together we right him

he is weak, unsteady on his five feet
and barely moves a hair or two along
before stumbling to rest
his head not aloft but bent to earth
his sixth leg dragging
his five others feeble
his wings without power

in slow motion he drifts onto his side
still, but for tiny jerking motions
of his long jointed legs

I try to read his face if he has one
and wonder if he seeks comfort ... or readies to die

I am now become hospice
watch him carefully for signs of life:
now and then a gasp or shiver
miniscule movements

I imagine the tiny shudders are his life's last
and wonder if he hurts
and rue I have not the wherewithal
to ease insect pain

my previously unattached curiosity
is now confronted by my compassion
merciful euthanasia comes to mind
I could do it quick and easy
with the slightest stomp

but when is the right time?

seeking clues from his body language
I remain unsure
how can I tell what is best for him?
how could I know his desire
        if he had one?
should I just let nature, as they say,
        take its course?
or should I put him out of his misery,
        if it is that?

I have become ineffably bound to him
this nameless once-soaring insect wonder
now tottering on the cusp
hymnoptera and mammal
I am he and he is me

in the long and shaky silence of uncertainty
together we face the mystery

The next four poems were written after being hospitalized for five broken ribs from a car accident when I was 88. The first poem, written two days after the accident, was found after my return home, scribbled on the back of a lunch menu from the trauma unit, where I had shared a room.

trauma unit

time is measured in
        millimeters of pain
each labored breath
        a gratitude

beyond the curtain
        an affirmation of tomorrow
skin is redundant
        your win is mine

reach for water
        beyond reach
        a macabre game

the 3 a.m. awakening
        from tiny precious dip into sleep
for vitals
        another airbag crushing
        while saving

pain bath of survival
        now easing
the long road of patience
        stretches ahead

teach me how
to use my pain
        to not use me

This second poem was written five days after the accident, while still in trauma unit, when pain-killing medications made ordinary mental processes a challenge to maintain.

trauma unit 2

morning stirs

reflection

awakens

something cosmic

old radio
plays jazz

its timelessness

provides

connection

This third poem was written eight days after the accident, while in rehab hospital. The relief of knowing I'd survived was mixed with the continuing pain of recovery, and the unexpected and unending support and practical help from an army of friends and poet/writer acquaintances.

impact

though pain waits
on the floor of my every breath
I ride there joyfully
on each wrenching sob
of gratitude

I savor every inspiration
that takes me
to that deepest fire pit
of life
where dwells the heart

for love has shown his face to me
from known and unknown crannies

and I am now as sure
as breath is life
that when all is done
I want to die into
        that place
                from which love
                        and poetry spring

This last poem, written the day before my discharge from the rehab unit, was found months later, scrawled on the inside book cover of a book I'd been gifted.

trauma nurse

her blue iceland eyes
looking through me
reveal nothing behind them

but the fear in her words
you look pale to me, unsteady
put on the belt
so you don't fall

machine gun instructions
tether me to her

newly disabled
by her security belt
I am led back
to my bed

I had been acing
my balancing tests for days
was steady, not unsure

then I learned
about the man
who fell on her watch
and died

wordlessly she turns back
to her medicine cart
to dispense healing
from her closed soul

At age 89, three weeks after moving in to Friends House, after reading three poems at 100 Thousand Poets, I experienced a severe shortness of breath and exhaustion. Fortunately, a fellow participant, a physician, recognized the symptoms and rushed me to an emergency room, saving my life.

air

1. air hunger

the air
seems to constantly slip away
even as I grasp for it
gasp for it
greedily gulping
never enough

I need to toughen my heart
I say

keep moving they say
it will come back

plodding for it feels like
plodding against it
I am Sisyphus exhausted

I seek it   I need it   I require it
desperately

but enough is never there
it eludes me
it never comes back

and I am drowning
again
oh not again

as that awful familiar darkness drops
black curtain
obliterating all

2. heart failure

your heart failed you
they said

how could it?
I asked
I love my heart
and it loves me

overworked exhausted
it gave out
they said

but all I did was
take care of the old lady
I'm to become
declutter   downsize
say too many final goodbyes
too fast
sell my beloved home
no time to grieve

move
leave
no time for reprieve
set up anew
where abode was fresh
but home yet alien
the heart hauling burdens
beyond its muscles' pull

until it could not
carry itself
from step to step
screaming
it's not enough
I need more air
where is the air?

3. savior

she dropped
out of the universe
of strangers
singing her heart
into our souls
and took the empty chair
beside my innocence

we made each other laugh
different as we were
she tall
lank
gorgeously chocolate
young

I stubby
white and wrinkled
almost used up

yet we knew unspoken things together
same eyes
seeing
the good things
the rest our challenge

our goodnights were not ready
my air starvation taking hold
she stayed the course
knew my need
insisted her aid
against my fear
took me
where I needed to go

Photo by Geri Cross

Eki Shola Abrams, M.D.

4. deliverance

once more was I pulled
back from the black edge
through the slim channel of life
into the world of light
and breath
the chain of days dented
but unbroken

once more
am I still
among the breathing
among the bleeding
marinated in gratitude

sponging up this universe
of strangers become saviors
saviors become friends

seeing anew
the daVinci face
in the lab waiting room
the Norman Rockwell old man
with his *bishon frise* puppy
and mint ice cream cone
the O'Keefe blossom
on my doorstep

gulping wonderment
in the splash of birdflight
awe with the mystery
of seed
life
in the once again miracle
of air

mirrors and glass

I stand in a room of mirrors and glass

reflections stop me
turn me in upon myself
farther   farther in
dense terrain
where all that was
resides entrapped in silken web

I stand in a room of mirrors and glass

transparencies pull me through
beyond the edge of sight
farther   farther out
past the rim of image
where the yet-to-be
waits

I stand in a room of mirrors and glass

where the yet-to-be
and all that was
invisibly intersect

the unanswerable

whisp'ring ghosts interred

in brain marrow

two fearsome questions

how soon

how

the obvious

not at this moment

Photo by Geri Cross

Turning 90
January 17, 2017

About the Author

After a stint as physician's wife and writing partner in the 1950s, Vilma's career for the next four decades was as a psychotherapist in Wisconsin, a calling which brought her, nearing retirement, to northern California in the early 1990s.

As someone who wrote poetry on the side since third grade, she turned to writing in earnest late in life, and became active in the Healdsburg Literary Guild in about 2001, serving on its Board for 15 years and hosting its monthly Third Sunday Salon from 2006 through 2014.

She was named the fifth **Healdsburg Literary Laureate**, serving in **2008/2009.**

In 2004, at age 77, she published the first of her six books of poetry, ***Colors of Glass***, followed by ***Murmurs & Outcries*** 2007, ***Snake Pit*** 2010, ***I Don't Know How to Do This, poems on aging*** 2011, ***making noise*** 2013, and ***90 is the new*** 2018.

Her work has appeared in anthologies *Present at the Creation*, 2006, *A Day in the Life of Healdsburg*, 2007, *Sometimes in the Open*, 2009, *When the Muse Calls*, 2009, *Continent of Light*, 2011, *World of Change*, 2014, *Cry of the Nightbird*, 2014, and *Healdsburg and Beyond*, 2016.

She has read in many local and area venues, and is proud to support the global peace and justice movement, 100 Thousand Poets for Change.

She has completed her first two volumes of memoir for her family, ***When the Iris Blooms*** 2012, and ***Mostly Roses*** 2015, and soon, her latest memoir tentatively untitled will join them. A fourth, covering the three to four decades of her career, is in progress.

Shortly after turning 90, she established, with poet friend Clare Morris, a monthly poetry venue, the Second Thursday PoetryPlus evening, in her new home, Friends House, a Quaker-inspired retirement community in Santa Rosa, California, where her gratitudes continue to accumulate.

Contact: vilmaginz@aol.com

Made in the USA
Las Vegas, NV
30 July 2023